COOPER'S PACK™

SEATTLE

by kyle & groot

Cooper's Pack Publishing

The Space Needle

My old friend Elliott invited me over to the city to hang out with him for the day.

Plus he said he had a surprise for me ...how could I say no?

I boarded the ferry and was off to Seattle for a new adventure.

Ahoy there, Elliott!

Elliott texted to meet on the waterfront at *Ivar's*.

Knowing Elliott, he's probably trying to score some fish (although their clam chowder is super tasty too).

There he is!

Ivar

Crazy Big Seagull

"Hey Cooper, great to see you," he said.

"And you Elliott...how's my favorite otter? You mentioned something about a surprise?" I hinted.

"We'll get to that later. It's a beautiful day out so let's take in some of the sites, maybe even catch a few snacks."

We headed off down the waterfront to see what we could find.

We popped into the **Seattle Aquarium** for a visit.

Check out the daily Diver Shows
and Underwater Dome Feeding.

After saying hello to Elliott's "people" at the *Aquarium*, we walked up the hill towards *Pike Place Market*.

Despite my prying, Elliott would not disclose the surprise.

"You'll see. For now, let's check out the seafood," he said.

Hmph!

Elliott helped himself to some oysters.

I tried the fresh raspberries.

Pike Place Market is a must-visit for food, fish, flowers, and fun. Say hi to the brass pig!

ARKET THEATER

presents **GROOVY STYLIN'S** crumpetlive.com

WORLD'S GREATEST BANK ROBBERY
WITH OLYMPIC THE ORIGINAL

11' 3"

Post Alley

I kept pestering Elliott about the surprise but he would not budge.

So instead, we decided to add an offering to one of Seattle's stickier "attractions", the **Wall of Gum**.

Yes, the **Wall of Gum.**

Leave your favorite flavor on the wall.

"When in Rome," Elliott said.

"When in Seattle," I corrected.

15

Gumless, we continued on our journey.

We headed down 1st Avenue and caught up on stories and jokes.

Elliott told me about his new job at the **Space Needle**.

"Sounds super cool," I said. "We should go there today."

"Definitely," Elliott agreed, with a smile on his face. "I think you will like it."

We walked past the **Seattle Art Museum** and the hardest working man in Seattle (you'll know when you see him).

Also visit **S.A.M.'s Olympic Sculpture Park** near **Pier 70**...great outdoor art!

We found ourselves in front of the **Seattle Public Library**...one of the coolest buildings in all of Seattle (and the world).

It is a great place to wander around and explore if you have the time.

Oh, and it is ideal for reading your favorite travel guides!

The **Central Library** has almost 10,000 windows (enough to cover 5-1/2 football fields)!

Secret passage to...?

19

We stopped by one of my favorite "secret squirrel" spots in all of Seattle... **Rainier Tower**'s rooftop park.

"As a pup I used to throw rubber bouncy balls off the wall here," I told Elliott.

"Guess what I always carry in my pack?"

"Game on!" Elliott exclaimed.

The "Popsicle" Building.

The park is a perfect spot to see the history of Seattle's buildings.

As we approached Seattle's shopping district near **Westlake Park**, we decided to have a beverage.

Walk-through fountain.

Like taking a shower without getting wet!

I had a half-caf, decaf mochachino latte (whatever that is).

As you can imagine, Elliott had a shrimp cocktail.

"Let's take the **Monorail** to **Seattle Center**," I suggested.

Elliott grinned. "A grand idea for sure, Coop. Let's do it!"

We headed up and got our tickets.

The **Monorail** goes right through **EMP**.

We were whisked away from downtown and arrived in **Seattle Center** a couple minutes later.

Get the front seat if you can!

We exited the **Monorail** and decided to amble about and see what looked interesting.

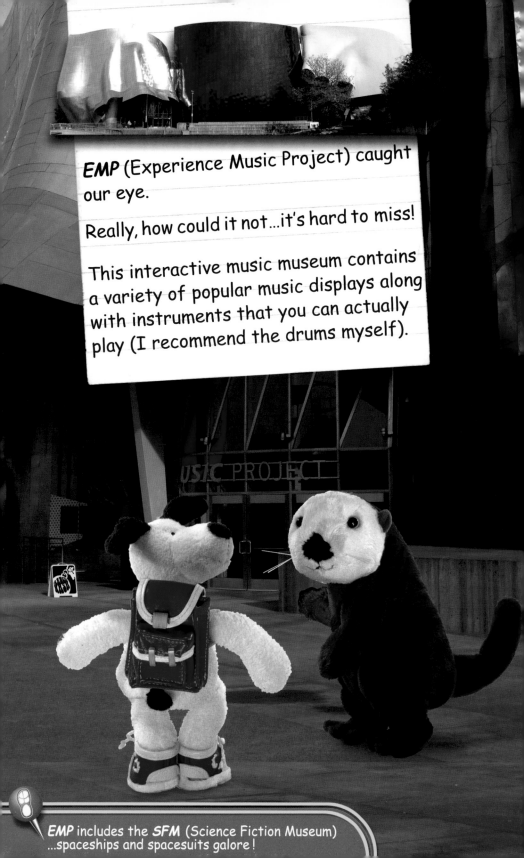

EMP (Experience Music Project) caught our eye.

Really, how could it not...it's hard to miss!

This interactive music museum contains a variety of popular music displays along with instruments that you can actually play (I recommend the drums myself).

EMP includes the **SFM** (Science Fiction Museum) ...spaceships and spacesuits galore!

They have a virtual *Soundgarden* of Seattle's music history including *Hendrix, Heart, Pearl Jam,* and others.

You can even see the *Presidents of the United States of America.*

Nirvana to my ears!

29

From across the street we could hear the sound of ducks.

In fact it was the **Ride the Ducks** tour.

How could we resist riding a duck?

We purchased our tickets and jumped onboard!

All aboard...!

Driving on the lake in a **Duck**...who knew?

The tour goes throughout Seattle and you get to boat on *Lake Union* (all in the same vehicle!).

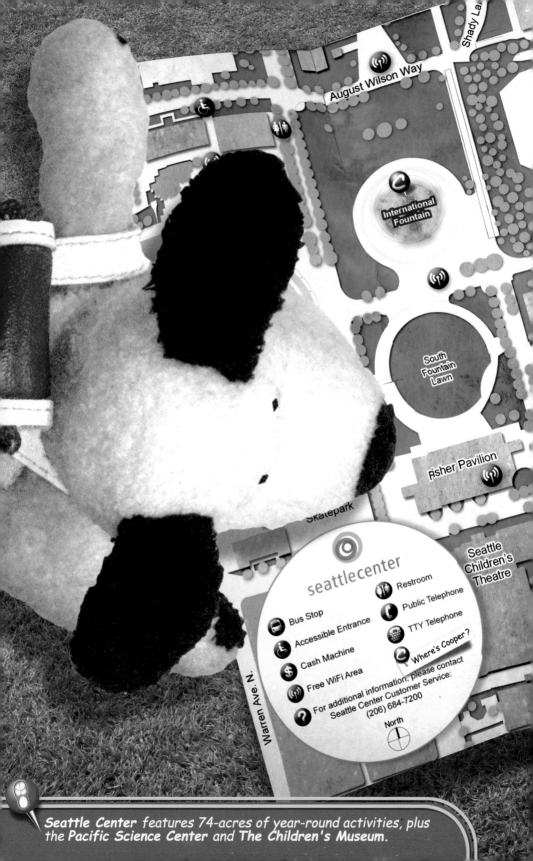

Shady La

August Wilson Way

International Fountain

South Fountain Lawn

Fisher Pavilion

Skatepark

Seattle Children's Theatre

Warren Ave. N.

seattlecenter

- Bus Stop
- Accessible Entrance
- Cash Machine
- Free WiFi Area
- ?

- Restroom
- Public Telephone
- TTY Telephone
- Where's Cooper ?

For additional information, please contact Seattle Center Customer Service: (206) 684-7200

North

Seattle Center features 74-acres of year-round activities, plus the **Pacific Science Center** and **The Children's Museum**.

After the tour, we wandered back into the Center and located a map.

Elliott had kept quiet about the surprise for way too long and I had to remind him not to forget it.

He pointed, "It's not far from here Cooper. You'll see soon enough." :)

My eagerness for the surprise had to wait a little longer as Elliott wanted to check out the **International Fountain**.

There is no better place to play in water on a hot Seattle day (...it gets hot here!).

After I took Elliott's picture, he suggested we head over to the **Space Needle** for lunch.

"It's about time! You've been nibbling on seafood all day," I reminded him.

"L~t's go!"

"There's where my new job is,"
Elliott pointed out.

"And perhaps a surprise," he added.

Did I mention how I love surprises?

Elliott helped me purchase a ticket and we were off to the top.

Elliott shared some *Space Needle* facts:

Built for the 1962 World's Fair and hosts over 1 million people a year.

← 605ft. high

← Observation Deck 520ft.

Revolving SkyCity
Restaurant 500ft.

3 Elevators:
Go as fast as 10mph and
will make the journey in
43 seconds.

← SkyLine Banquet
Facility 100ft.

← SpaceBase

There is the **EMP** and **Monorail** tunnel!

The original name of the **Space Needle** was **The Space Cage** - glad they changed it ;)

Lake Union

We stopped on the restaurant level and sat down for a quick lunch.

You can probably guess what Elliott ordered.

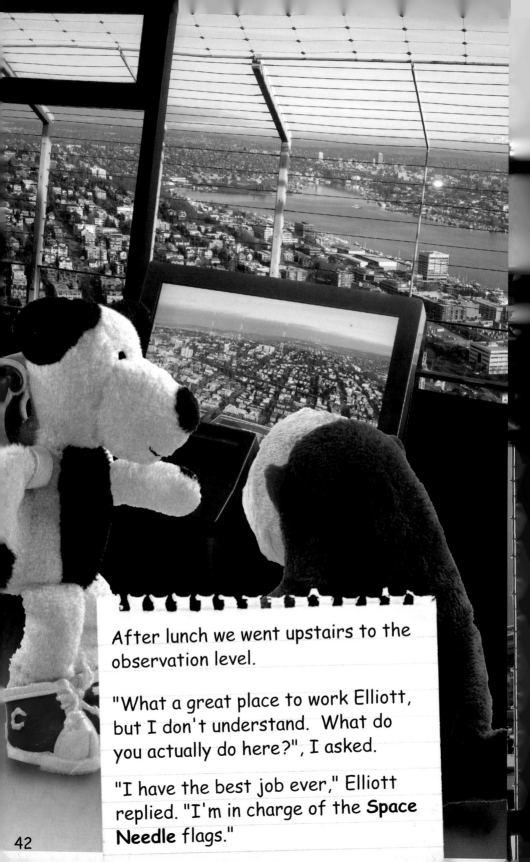

After lunch we went upstairs to the observation level.

"What a great place to work Elliott, but I don't understand. What do you actually do here?", I asked.

"I have the best job ever," Elliott replied. "I'm in charge of the **Space Needle** flags."

Elliott Bay

Queen Anne Hill

He explained how they fly many different flags, depending upon local events, sports teams, and for fun.

Very cool indeed I thought.

43

Elliott led me outside to the observation deck where we could see **Mount Rainier**, several islands on the **Puget Sound**, **Lake Union**, **Lake Washington**, and even other cities.

"I can't believe how big Seattle is! It goes on forever."

44

"You should see it from the top," Elliott replied.

"There's more?"

"Come with me oh wise dog. You haven't seen anything yet--or maybe you have?" he added with a grin.

Elliott led me through a hidden door where I looked up to see the steepest stairway I'd ever seen.

"My new job, and your surprise, are up there," he pointed.

We climbed the stairway and Elliott popped open the hatch.

We were on the tippy top of the *Space Needle!!!*

Elliott tugged on the lines to a flag with my initial on it.

"I had this made especially for you Cooper."

"This is the coolest thing I have ever seen," I replied in awe. "You rock, Elliott!"

"Anytime you see your flag waving from the top of the Space Needle, you will know I am thinking of my good friend."

"Thank you so much for the great surprise. I can't believe you get to work on the "roof" of the **Space Needle**, and they gave you a helicopter to boot!"

50

Ellicopter pad.

"I like to call it my Ellicopter," Elliott replied.

"Come on...let's take the fun way down!"

51

"Hold on tight!" Elliott exclaimed.

The Ellicopter whirled away as we headed down to the ground below.

Another great day in Seattle was complete.

More to Explore:

Places I visited:

1. Waterfront
2. Seattle Aquarium
3. Pike Place Market
4. Wall of Gum
5. Seattle Art Museum
6. Seattle Public Library
7. Rainier Tower Rooftop Park
8. Westlake Park
9. Monorail
10. EMP
11. Ride the Ducks
12. Seattle Center
13. International Fountain
14. Space Needle

MERCER ST

SEATTLE CENTER

BROAD ST

5TH AVE N

JOH

DEN

S.A.M. SCULPTURE PARK

PIER 70

BELLTOV

ELLIOTT BAY
(Puget Sound

YOU ARE HERE

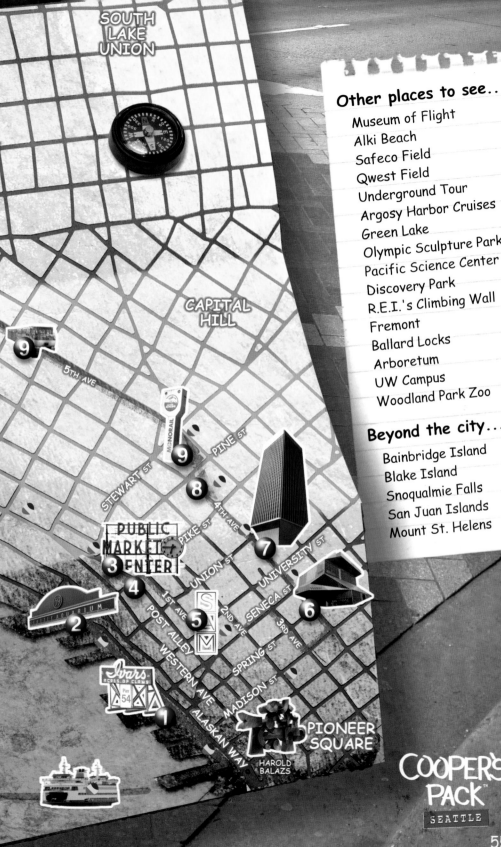

SOUTH LAKE UNION

CAPITAL HILL

5TH AVE

MONORAIL

PINE ST

STEWART ST

PIKE ST

4TH AVE

PUBLIC MARKET CENTER

UNION ST

UNIVERSITY ST

1ST AVE

POST ALLEY

2ND AVE

SENECA ST

3RD AVE

SPRING ST

WESTERN AVE

MADISON ST

Ivars
ACRES OF CLAMS
Pier 54

ALASKAN WAY

PIONEER SQUARE

HAROLD BALAZS

Other places to see...

Museum of Flight
Alki Beach
Safeco Field
Qwest Field
Underground Tour
Argosy Harbor Cruises
Green Lake
Olympic Sculpture Park
Pacific Science Center
Discovery Park
R.E.I.'s Climbing Wall
Fremont
Ballard Locks
Arboretum
UW Campus
Woodland Park Zoo

Beyond the city...

Bainbridge Island
Blake Island
Snoqualmie Falls
San Juan Islands
Mount St. Helens

COOPER'S PACK

SEATTLE

More to Explore: Did You Know?

What makes Seattle unique?

Mt. Rainier

Puget Sound

Space Needle

Pike Place Market

Boeing airplane testing

Washington State Ferry System

Rain (hey, it doesn't rain that much!)

Two Mountain Ranges:
Cascades to the East
Olympics to the West

Seattle has many annual festivals, including:

Seattle Maritime Festival (Tug Boat Races!)

Bite of Seattle (Seattle Center)

Folklife Festival (Memorial Day)

Bumbershoot (Labor Day)

Seafair (across the city)

Solstice Parade (in Fremont)

BRAZIL'S BEST

Be in the know!

-Visit Pike Place Market (not Pike's Place Market), or simply "The Market".

-UW ("U-Dub") University of Washington.

-The Washington State Ferry System is the largest in the nation (3rd in the world).

-Seattle is originally named after a local Indian chief, Chief Sealth.

-Seattleites buy more sunglasses (per capita) than any other city in the nation (who says it rains that much!).

-"Skid row" was originally named after an area in Seattle where logs were slid down the hill during timber harvesting. This later became a common phrase describing a down-and-out area of any city.

-Seattle is nicknamed the "Emerald City" due to the amount of evergreen trees in the region.

-The Columbia Tower is Seattle's tallest building (12th in the nation) at 76 stories.

-Evergreen Point floating bridge is the world's longest floating bridge (yes, and it's made from cement!).

-Cooper lives on Bainbridge Island.

-Seattle is also known as the Jet City. Can you guess why?

-The former Seafirst Bank building on 4th and Madison St. is nicknamed "the box the Space Needle came delivered in".

-There are 25 lightning rods located on top of the Space Needle (24 plus the actual tower).

-The world's largest building (Boeing's final assembly plant) is located just north of Seattle.

COOPER'S
PACK
SEATTLE

57

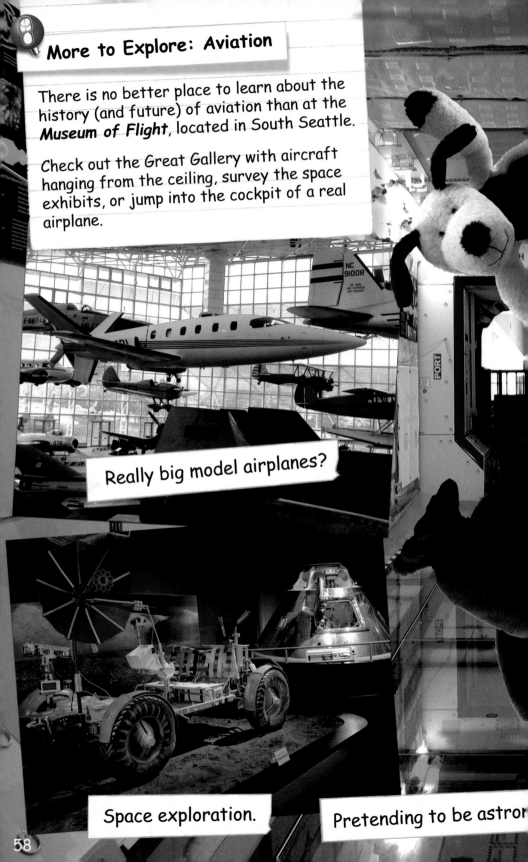

More to Explore: Aviation

There is no better place to learn about the history (and future) of aviation than at the **Museum of Flight**, located in South Seattle.

Check out the Great Gallery with aircraft hanging from the ceiling, survey the space exhibits, or jump into the cockpit of a real airplane.

Really big model airplanes?

Space exploration.

Pretending to be astror

Original Air Force One.

Cockpit of the Concorde.

Jet City Aviation Activities:

- Explore the **Museum of Flight**'s exhibits including the Concorde, the first Air Force One, and even a moon buggy. HINT: Go in the Control Tower!

- See a brand new Boeing 737 on a train. HINT: Often you will see them next to the **Olympic Sculpture Park**, near **Pier 70**.

- Watch the seaplanes take-off and land from **South Lake Union**. HINT: Take a flight to the **San Juan Islands** from here.

Space Station Lab.

COOPER'S PACK™

SEATTLE

59

More to Explore: Rain or Shine

Seattle is known as the city of rain, showers, and drizzle yet does it really rain that much?

As you can see from the chart to the right, it rains more per year in many places you may not have considered.

However, as noted from local meteorologists, this is because it doesn't rain very heavily in Seattle compared to other places.

Overall you will often hear the forecast calling for "showers with sun breaks".

Considering the amount of boating and outdoor activities in Seattle, Cooper doesn't think Seattle deserves the bad rap...go sun!

AVERAGE RAIN FALL PER YEAR (in inches)*

Hong Kong	86"
Tokyo	60"
Miami	58"
Bangkok	57"
Atlanta	50"
Zurich	42"
Boston	42"
New York	42"
Milan	38"
Seattle	38"

*Compiled from a variety of sources. Measurements approximate.

If you watch the local weather report, they use some interesting words to describe rain.

What do they really mean...?

Rain: Precipitation larger than 0.5 mm in diameter.

Drizzle: Many small drops of water (droplets less than 0.5 mm in diameter).

Sprinkles: Light rain.

Showers: Rain from a series of cumulonimbus clouds (often sudden and dense rain).

Isolated Showers: Smaller area of showers.

Scattered Showers: Larger area of showers.

Intermittent Showers: Precipitation that starts and stops at irregular intervals.

Downpours: Heavy rain.

Sleet: Rain that freezes before it hits ground.

COOPER'S PACK

SEATTLE

Often called the **Emerald City**, Seattle's history is rooted in the natural resources, geographic location, and people of the Northwestern United States.

From logging in the 1850s, airplane production in the 1940s, and the technology boom in the 1980s, all of these events have added to Seattle's unique legacy.

Seattle was named after **Chief Seattle** (also called Chief Sealth), a local Indian chief who was well-known for his wisdom and help during a time of settlement and logging expansion in the 1850s.

Almost the entire downtown (including the waterfront wharves) burnt down in the **Great Seattle Fire of 1889**.

Luckily citizens were able to rebuild the city of more durable brick and mortar (a lesson learned by many of the world's great cities).

The **Klondike Gold Rush** of the late 19th century brought thousands of people to Seattle, as a way-station to find gold in Canada.

This created many new jobs and helped boost the city's infrastructure.

As the city grew into the 1900s, a little airplane company was founded on **Lake Union** by William Boeing.

Boeing supplied the Allies' with many of the bombers used during World War II (over 350 a month!) and became the world's largest aircraft manufacturer (and Cooper's favorite airplanes in which to fly...especially the 747).

In preparation for the *1962 World's Fair*, Seattle built the **Space Needle, Monorail**, and much of the present-day **Seattle Center**.

The futuristic-themed fair forever branded Seattle's skyline with the iconic **Space Needle**.

As the 1980s introduced personal computers to the masses, Bill Gates and Paul Allen were developing what would become the world's most profitable company, Microsoft.

Their "windows" view of computing forever changed the technological landscape of Seattle (and the world!).

Other notable Seattle companies include Starbucks (the first Starbucks is located in **Pike Place Market**), Costco, Nordstrom, REI, Amazon, Ivar's, Cooper's Pack, and more.

ADULTS

ARTHUR A
DENNY
AND WIFE

JOHN N. LOW
AND WIFE

CARSON D BOREN
AND WIFE

At this place
on 13 November 1851
there landed from
the Schooner Exact
Captain Folger the
little colony which
developed into the
City of Seattle

WILLIAM N BELL
AND WIFE

LOUISA BOREN

DAVID T. DENNY

CHARLES C TERRY

LEE TERRY

ON THIS SPOT
SOME YEARS
AGO A BONE
WAS BURIED
BY EXPLORER
GF COOPER

BIRTHPLACE
OF SEATTLE

"NEW YORK-ALK

COOPER'S
PACK
SEATTLE

63

That really is a **Pink Elephant**!

Pig Art

Duck into Lake Union.

More to Explore: Cooper's Photos

Remember to take pictures of the places you visit and the things you like.

Safeco Field

Pacific Science Center

Gas Works Park

PIKE PLACE MARKET

COOPER'S PACK™
SEATTLE

Learning to fly at the **Museum of Flight**.

Sound support for the home team...!

Full contact drumming at *EMP*.

More to Explore: Out and About

Big Cooper working the Seattle scene...

Digging the clam at **Ivar's.**

Top o' the **Needle...!**

Rocking it at **REI.**

Captain Cooper on a **Duck.**

COOPER'S PACK™
SEATTLE

67

COOPER

Eye Color: Black
Born: Olympic Mountains
(outside of Seattle, WA)
Home: Bainbridge Island

Favorites:
Foods: T-bone Steak, Milk
Color: Navy blue
Places: Hiking, Pacific Ocean,
Grandpa's house
Books: A Separate Peace
Artist: Marcus Bausch, Jr.
Teacher: Mr. Axling (Geography)
Class: Geography, Languages
Music: Tragically Hip, Beatles
Sports: Soccer, Skiing, Boating
Hobbies: Traveling, Writing
Sayings: "Top Dog", "You rock!"
Nicknames: Coop

Elliott

Eye Color: Blue
Born: Pudget Sound
  (Elliott Bay in Seattle)
Home: Seattle

Favorites:
Foods: Penn Cove Oysters, Crab
Color: Sky Blue, Yellow
Places: Puget Sound,
  Top of the Needle
Books: <u>The Call of the Wild</u>
Artist: Joan Miró, Harold Balazs
Teacher: Mr. Layton
Class: Social Studies, Swimming
Music: Sweet Water, Miles Davis
Sports: Deep Sea Diving, Fishing
Hobbies: Flying, Collecting Flags
Sayings: "Sterling"
Nickname: Elli

Insert your photo here.

Name:

Height:

Weight:

Eye Color:

Born:

Languages:

Favorites:
Places:

Books:

Music:

Sayings:

70 Nickname:

Insert photo of your traveling buddy or the city you visited here.

Travel Information:

Date: _____

Destination(s): _____

_____

_____

_____

Transportation: _____

_____

_____

_____

_____

More to Explore: A Bit About You

COOPER'S PACK™
SEATTLE

Don't forget to add your own drawings.

Send Cooper your travel stories, highlights and photos of your stuffed animal friend(s) to: **Cooper@CoopersPack.com**

You may find them featured on Cooper's website, including updates and additional pictures of Cooper's adventures.

Credits / Acknowledgements:

REI
Experience Music Project
Ride the Ducks of Seattle
Seattle Art Museum
Seattle Sounders FC
Seattle Aquarium
Seattle Center Monorail
Seattle Public Library
Pike Place Market PDA
Seattle Center
Space Needle Corporation
Ivar's Seafood Restaurants
Seattle Mariners / Ben Van Houten
Scott Sistek / KOMO News
Jeff Renner / King 5
Washington State DOT Ferries Division

Additional imagery provided by the Museum of Flight:
Original Air Force One. - Jim Anderson
Cockpit of the Concorde. - The Museum of Flight
Space exploration. - Heath Moffatt

kyle
Enjoys driving his boat, especially in the sun.

groot
Enjoys riding his bike even in the rain.